Piano / Vocal / Guitar

TWILA PARIS - TWENTY FAVORITES

ISBN 0-7935-7857-4

HAL•LEONARD®
CORPORATION

7777 W. BLUEMOUND RD. P.O. BOX 13819 MILWAUKEE, WI 53213

Visit Hal Leonard Online at
www.halleonard.com

TWILA PARIS - TWENTY FAVORITES

MY FAVORITE SONGS ... AND WHY

1. Bonded Together – One morning when Jack and I were first married, my dad showed up at our house excited about his quiet time. He shared with us what God had just revealed to him about being truly "bonded together" with Christ and all that it means to a believer. By the time he left, we were excited, too.

2. Carry the Light – In 1988, over 100 Christian artists came together to record this song. It was a statement of our commitment to take an active role in reaching the world with the message of Jesus Christ. I am grateful that it has also served as a continuing encouragement to others who share the same commitment.

3. Every Heart That Is Breaking – A few years ago, we heard from a friend that his wife of one year had left him. She said she had never loved him. Responding to his grief and devastation, I was reminded that there are, at any given moment, millions of breaking hearts all over the world. And God is always waiting with open arms to comfort any one of us who will just reach out to Him.

4. Faithful Friend – I wrote this song for and with my friend Steven Curtis Chapman. It's about the principles involved in any Christian friendship. And it's also a commitment from us to the Body of Christ to be faithful to live what we say and sing.

5. Faithful Men – To be faithful on a given day may not seem to have great significance, but over a lifetime, simple faithfulness will yield great fruit for the Kingdom of God. (A quote from my dad, "My faithfulness plus God's faithfulness equals success.")

6. God Is in Control – One day while driving to my mom's house a few years ago, I was thinking about the circumstances of the world and I began to be filled with anxiety. Almost immediately God reminded me that ultimately, all authority in heaven and earth belongs to Him. I began to sing as I drove and by the time I got back home, the chorus was finished.

7. He Is Exalted – One of the most fulfilling things I experience as a writer is the knowledge that some of the songs I've been given by God are being returned to Him in worship by people who don't know my name, in languages I've never heard and in places I may never go. "He is Exalted", perhaps more than any other song, has traveled the world without me.

8. A Heart That Knows You – Left on my own, I would probably always turn away from the most difficult circumstances. But throughout my life, God has loved me enough to take me by the hand and lead me down the paths that He knew would build His character in me. It's His responsibility to lay the plans for our lives. It's our responsibility to trust Him and submit to His will — even when we don't understand it. His love and wisdom will inevitably be demonstrated by the end result.

9. Honor and Praise – Sometimes doing menial tasks frees the mind to hear God and inspires creativity. This song was entirely written in the shower. No wonder it takes me so long to get ready ...

10. How Beautiful – God wants us to love one another in the same way we love Him. I've long understood the importance of unity among believers, but a few years ago God began to give me an actual emotional, familial love for the members of His body; those I knew and those I didn't. This song was the result.

11. I Am Not Afraid Anymore – Most of us have a tendency to believe we are trusting God completely while we are actually holding back areas that are "too important" to trust even to Him. God has such a gentle, yet determined way of proving to us, one area at a time, that we really can and must trust Him with our whole lives. An interesting result is that each time we relinquish control of a particular area, we also relinquish the related fear.

12. Joy of the Lord – This song was written while I was washing dishes – which I've always thought is a testimony to the truth of its message.

13. Lamb of God – This is one of my favorites of all the songs I've "written" because it's about who God is, what He's done and who we are called to be in response; the Gospel at its core.

14. Prince of Peace – This is a song of intercession. It was written in 1986. It occurs to me that this prayer seems even more timely today.

15. Runner – I co-wrote this song with my sister Starla. Our home fellowship is the "Youth with a Mission" based in Arkansas. When we wrote the song, we were thinking specifically of missionaries, especially the ones we knew. But, of course, we are all called to "bear the flame," and the encouragement in this song is for every faithful child of God.

16. Sweet Victory – God brings victory to any struggle in His way and in His time. This song is about the fact that spiritual victory is always available and is even more important than the physical victory we are usually seeking.

17. The Time Is Now – This song was written for a Billy Graham crusade which was simulcast around the world in 1995. The message is timeless. The only hope for individuals and for society is Jesus Christ.

18. True Friend – One day, over ten years ago, my friend Jayne Farrell called me out of the blue just to encourage me. She couldn't have known, but I really needed encouragement at just that moment. God's love, whether in the form of affirmation or correction, is often shown to us through friends who are listening to Him.

19. The Warrior Is a Child – I almost didn't record this song. I thought perhaps it was just for me and others might not relate to the message. I couldn't have been more wrong. Over the years, I think I've received more response to this one song than to all the others combined – from children, pastors, grandmothers, etc. To me, it proves the commonality of our journey as Christians. No matter who we are, no matter what our role in the Kingdom, we are all children before the Lord, all in desperate need of His love and grace.

20. Watch and Pray – We have a very real enemy and we must be vigilant in every area of life, especially in light of the fact that Jesus is coming very soon and no one knows the day or the hour.

BONDED TOGETHER

Words and Music by
TWILA PARIS

1. Like a tight-ly wo-ven gar-ment, like a met-
2. There is nev-er space be-tween us for a sep-

-al al-loy;
-a-ra-tion;

We are put to-geth-
We are put to-geth-

CARRY THE LIGHT

Words and Music by
TWILA PARIS

In this world of dark — ness, we are giv — en ___
Count them by the dark mil — lions, blind — ed slaves to ___

light, Hope for all the dy — ing. ___
sin. In — side, all they are dy — ing. ___

How will __ they know? How will __ they know that
How will __ they know? How will __ they know that

EVERY HEART THAT IS BREAKING

Words and Music by
TWILA PARIS

FAITHFUL FRIEND

Words and Music by TWILA PARIS
and STEVEN CURTIS CHAPMAN

Female: Ev - 'ry - one knows ___ you as a man ___ of hon - or. I am glad ___ to know ___ you sim - ply as ___ a friend. ___ You've al - ways tak - en

FAITHFUL MEN

Words and Music by
TWILA PARIS

Come and join the reap - ers, All the king - dom seek - ers, Lay - ing down your life to find it in the end;

GOD IS IN CONTROL

Words and Music by
TWILA PARIS

This is— no time for fear. This is a time for— faith and de-
His- to- ry mar- ches on. There is— a bot- tom— line drawn a-

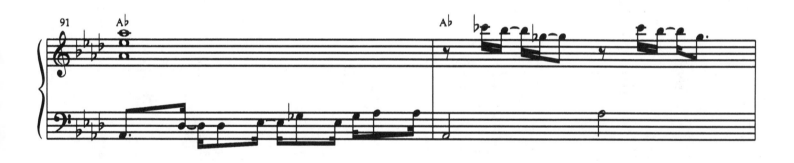

A HEART THAT KNOWS YOU

Words and Music by
TWILA PARIS

Thought I knew so much but I've got so much to learn.
You would ne-ver lead where You had not been.

Got so far to go,
E-very road I face,

still ce - le - brate,_____ fol - low - ing_____ love_____ through_____ the fire._____ the fire._____ It may__ be____ for my _____ sake just to help__ me__ grow._____

fol - low - ing —— love —————————

through the fire. ————————

HE IS EXALTED

Words and Music by
TWILA PARIS

Triumphant! ♩ = 168

He _____ is the ____ Lord, _____ for -

HONOR AND PRAISE

Words and Music by
TWILA PARIS

Right-eous and ho-ly, in all of Your
Fill-ing and the tem-ple, in the work of Your

ways;
grace; we come be-fore You with hon-or and

HOW BEAUTIFUL

Words and Music by
TWILA PARIS

I AM NOT AFRAID ANYMORE

Words and Music by
TWILA PARIS

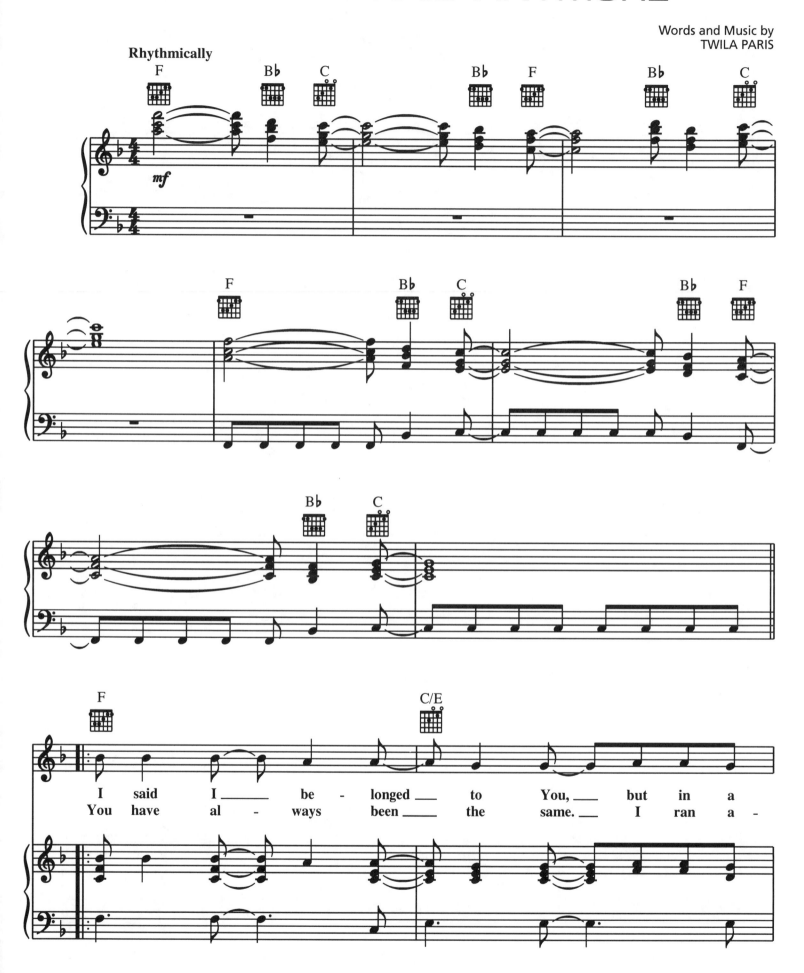

Rhythmically

I said I ___ be - longed ___ to You, ___ but in a
You have al - ways been ___ the same. ___ I ran a -

THE JOY OF THE LORD

Words and Music by
TWILA PARIS

The joy of— the Lord
joy of— the Lord

joy of— the Lord will be— my strength. I will— not wai - ver,

joy of— the Lord is— my strength. The

Repeat 4 x

LAMB OF GOD

Words and Music by
TWILA PARIS

Your on-ly Son no sin to hide, But You have sent Him from Your side

To walk up-on this guilt-y sod and to be-come the Lamb of

God. Your gift of love they cru-ci-

PRINCE OF PEACE

Words and Music by
TWILA PARIS

100

RUNNER

Words and Music by TWILA PARIS
and STARLA ORENE PARIS

Cour-i-er val-iant, bear-ing the flame,___
Ob-sta-cle an-cient, chill-ing the way,___

mes-sen-ger no-ble sent in His name;___ Fast-er and hard-er
en-e-my wak-ened stok-ing the fray;___ Still be de-ter-mined

run through the night,___ des-per-ate re-lay
fear-less and true,___ lift high the stand-ard

22 Asus A(2) Asus A(2) Asus A(2) *D.S. al Coda*

25 CODA A A(2)/C# Esus/D Esus Esus/D Esus N.C.

28 Esus/D E/D A(2)/C# Esus/D

Mind-ful of man-y wait-ing to run,___ des-tined to fin-

31 E/D A(2)/C# F#sus/E F#/E B(2)/D#

-ish what you've be-gun;___ Mil-lions be-fore___ you cheer-ing you on,

TRUE FRIEND

Words and Music by
TWILA PARIS

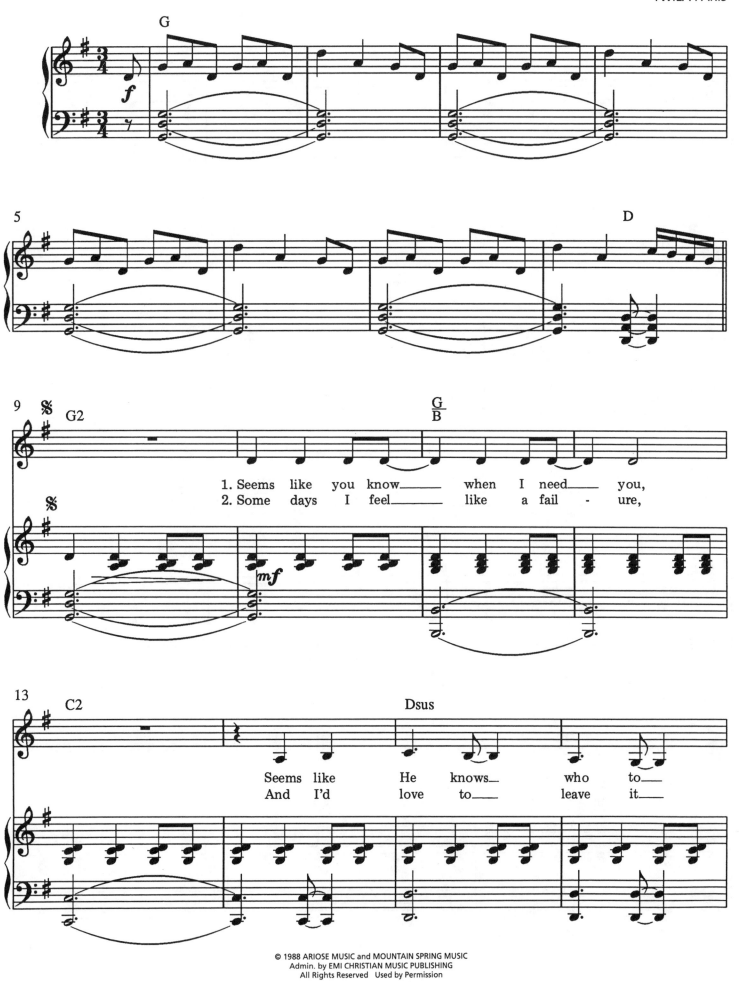

1. Seems like you know_____ when I need_____ you,
2. Some days I feel_____ like a fail - ure,

Seems like He knows_____ who to_____
And I'd love to_____ leave it_____

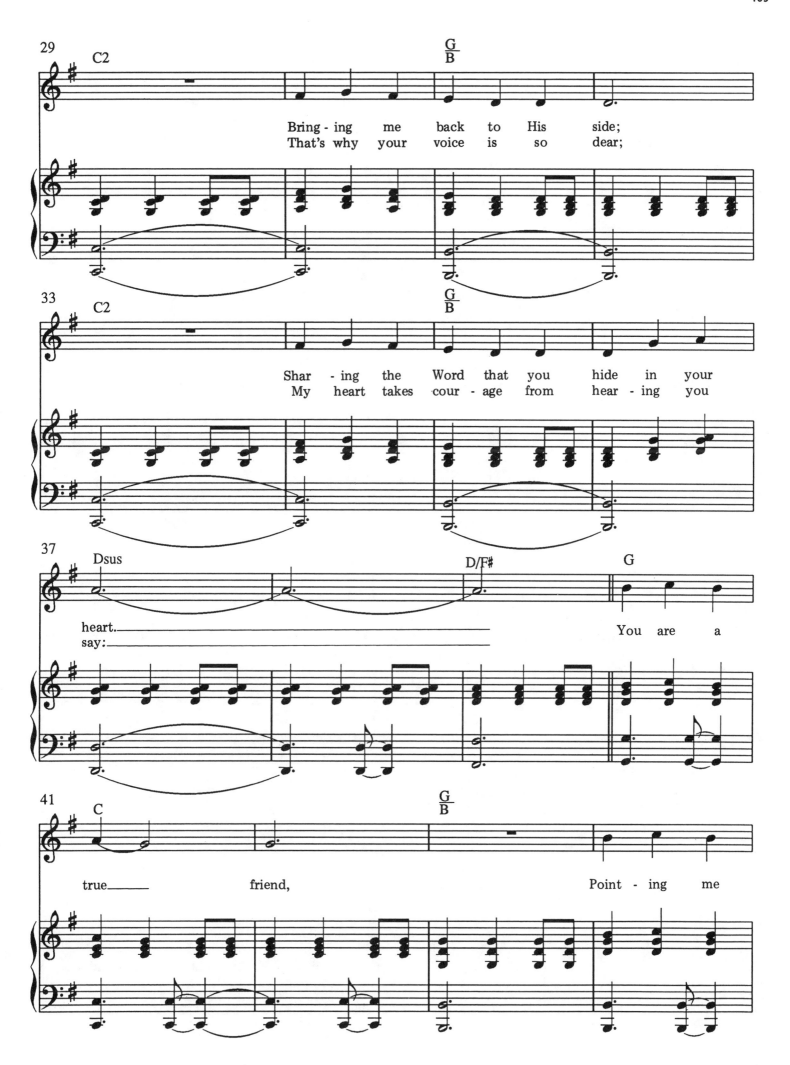

SWEET VICTORY

Words and Music by
TWILA PARIS

1. Qui- et- ly___ you lead___ me to___ an o-
2. In___ this place___ I rest___ in more___ than I

- pen place,___
___ can see,___

Hold___ me in___ the still-
High___ a- bove___ the tur-

ness till___ I see___ Your face;
bu- lence You car- ry me;

THE TIME IS NOW

Words and Music by
TWILA PARIS

WATCH AND PRAY

Words and Music by
TWILA PARIS

The e - ne - my roams like a roar - ing li - on,
The King will ap - pear with the shout of glo - ry,

look-ing for the sleep - ing,
all the earth a - wak - ing,

THE WARRIOR IS A CHILD

Words and Music by
TWILA PARIS